CAREERS IN THE
BUILDING TRADES

Electrician

Careers in the Building Trades

A Growing Demand

Apprenticeships

Carpenter

Construction & Building Inspector

Electrician

Flooring Installer

Heating and Cooling Technician

Masonry Worker

Plumber

Roofer

Working in Green Construction

CAREERS IN THE BUILDING TRADES

A GROWING DEMAND

Electrician

Andrew Morkes

MASON CREST

Mason Crest
450 Parkway Drive, Suite D
Broomall, Pennsylvania 19008
(866) MCP-BOOK (toll-free)
www.masoncrest.com

First printing

9 8 7 6 5 4 3 2 1

ISBN (hardback) 978-1-4222-4114-1

ISBN (series) 978-1-4222-4110-3

ISBN (ebook) 978-1-4222-7684-6

Cataloging-in-Publication Data on file with the Library of Congress

NATIONAL
HIGHLIGHTS

Developed and Produced by National Highlights Inc.
Proofreader: Mika Jin
Interior and cover design: Yolanda Van Cooten
Production: Michelle Luke

CONTENTS

KEY ICONS TO LOOK FOR:

Words to understand: These words with their easy-to-understand definitions will increase the reader's understanding of the text while building vocabulary skills.

Sidebars: This boxed material within the main text allows readers to build knowledge, gain insights, explore possibilities, and broaden their perspectives by weaving together additional information to provide realistic and holistic perspectives.

Educational Videos: Readers can view videos by scanning our QR codes, providing them with additional educational content to supplement the text. Examples include news coverage, moments in history, speeches, iconic sports moments and much more!

Text-dependent questions: These questions send the reader back to the text for more careful attention to the evidence presented there.

Research projects: Readers are pointed toward areas of further inquiry connected to each chapter. Suggestions are provided for projects that encourage deeper research and analysis.

Series glossary of key terms: This back-of-the-book glossary contains terminology used throughout this series. Words found here increase the reader's ability to read and comprehend higher-level books and articles in this field.

INTRODUCTION
The Trades: Great Careers, Good Money, and Other Rewards

Trades workers play a major role in the success of economies throughout the world. They keep the power on (electricians), build structures ranging from houses to skyscrapers (carpenters and ironworkers), and install and repair pipes that carry water, fuel, and other liquids to, from, and within businesses, factories, and homes (plumbers and pipefitters), among many other job duties. Yet despite their pivotal role in our society, only 6 percent of students consider a career in the trades, according to ExploretheT-rades.org. Why? Because many young people have misconceptions about the trades. They have been told that the trades are low-paying, lack job security, and other untruths. In fact, working in the trades is one of the best career choices you can make. The following paragraphs provide more information on why a career in the trades is a good idea.

Good pay. Contrary to public perception, skilled trades workers earn salaries that place them firmly in the middle class. For example, average annual salaries for electricians in the United States are $56,650, according to the U.S. Department of Labor. This salary is higher than the average earnings for some careers that require a bachelor's or graduate degree—including archivists ($54,570), meeting planners ($52,020), social workers ($50,710), counselors ($49,740), and recreational therapists ($48,190). Trades workers who become managers or who launch their own businesses can have earnings that range from $90,000 to $200,000.

Strong employment prospects. There are shortages of trades workers throughout the world, according to the human resource consulting firm ManpowerGroup. In fact, trades workers are the most in-demand occupational field in the Americas, Europe, the Middle East, and Africa. They ranked fourth in the Asia-Pacific region. Electricians are in especially strong demand in the United States, Norway, Russia, Canada, Australia, and New Zealand.

Provides a comfortable life without a bachelor's or graduate degree. For decades in the United States and other countries, there has been an emphasis on earning a college degree as the key to life success. But studies show that only 35 percent of future jobs in the United States will require a four-year degree or higher. With college tuition continuing to increase and the chances of landing a good job out of college decreasing, a growing number of people are entering apprenticeship programs to prepare for careers in the trades. And unlike college students, apprentices receive a salary while learning and they don't have to pay off loans after they complete their education. It's a good feeling to start your career without $50,000 to $200,000 in college loans.

Rewarding work environment and many career options. A career in the trades is fulfilling because you get to use both your hands and your head to solve problems and make the world a better place. You can work at a construction site, at a manufacturing plant, at a business, and in other settings. Many trades workers launch their own businesses.

Jobs can't be offshored. Trades careers involve hands-on work that requires the worker to be on-site to do his or her job. As a result, there is no chance that your position will be offshored to a foreign country. In an uncertain employment atmosphere, that's encouraging news.

Job opportunities are available throughout the United States and the world. There is a need for trades workers in small towns and big cities. If demand for their skills is not strong in their geographic area, they can move to other cities, states, or countries where demand is higher.

Are the Trades Right for Me?

Test your interest in the trades. How many of these statements do you agree with?

☐ My favorite class in school is shop.

☐ I like doing household repairs.

☐ I am fascinated by electronics.

☐ I like to use power and hand tools.

☐ I like projects that allow me to work with my hands.

☐ I enjoy observing work at construction sites.

☐ I like to build electronics and other things that require electricity.

☐ I like to build and fix things.

☐ I like to watch home-repair shows on TV and the internet.

☐ I don't mind getting my hands dirty.

☐ I am good at math.

☐ I like to figure out how things work.

If many of the statements above describe you, then you should consider a career in the trades. But you don't need to select a career right now. Check out this book on a career as an electrician and other books in the series to learn more about occupational paths in the trades. Good luck with your career exploration!

Words to Understand

circuit breaker: A device in a building or structure that stops the flow of excess current that may damage the electrical circuit.

current: A measure of electrical flow. It is measured in amperes.

electrical conduit: A tube that is used to protect and direct electrical wiring. It is made of metal, plastic, fiber, or fired clay.

National Electrical Code: A series of rules in the United States for safe electrical design, installation, and inspection that were developed by the National Fire Protection Association. The code has been adopted in all fifty states.

photovoltaic device: A type of technology that is used to generate electricity directly from sunlight via an electronic process.

self-employed: Working for oneself as a small business owner, rather than for a corporation or other employer. Self-employed people are responsible for generating their own income, and they must provide their own fringe benefits (such as health insurance).

CHAPTER 1

What Do Electricians Do?

We often take electricians for granted until the power goes out in our homes during a dark, stormy night, or we're otherwise without the power to run our refrigerators, grocery stores, and even electric vehicles. Electricians make the great invention of electricity possible. They install, maintain, and repair electrical and power systems in homes and businesses. They work in countless industries throughout the world—from manufacturing, construction, and broadcasting, to utilities, telecommunications, and transportation. To obtain their skills, aspiring electricians complete apprenticeships or training programs at technical schools. Others receive informal training from experienced electricians or through the military. Many cities, states, and countries require electricians to be licensed.

Some electricians work as members of large work crews to install the electrical components and systems for major construction or infrastructure projects such as the erection of a 100-story skyscraper or the construction of a new

■ *About 71 percent of electricians in the United States work in the construction industry.*

airport. Others ensure that the electrical systems at factories that manufacture smart phones, new cars, and countless other products, run smoothly. And still others operate their own businesses—installing and repairing home electrical systems, or working as a subcontractor at a construction site. Although their job duties vary,

A Little History

From the earliest days of recorded history, scientists theorized about and performed basic experiments with electricity. Although breakthroughs and discoveries were made throughout the centuries, it was not until 1800, when an Italian scientist named Alessandro Volta created the first electric cell, that the study of electricity really took off. Some major breakthroughs that occurred in the decades thereafter include:

- the recognition of electromagnetism (1819–1820)
- the invention of the electric motor (1821)
- the discovery of the principles of electromagnetism induction, generation, and transmission (1831)
- the demonstration of the first constant electric light (1835).

These and other discoveries led to the founding of the Edison Electric Light Co. in the United States and American Electric and Illuminating in Canada in 1878. A year later, the first commercial power station opened in San Francisco. Within a few years, commercially available supplies of electricity began changing the way people lived—lighting homes that were once lit by candlelight and gas lamps and greatly increasing production at factories. These developments further fueled the Industrial Revolution. In 1900, fewer than 10 percent of U.S. families had access to electricity. Today, 100 percent of U.S. families have access to electricity. On the other hand, an estimated 1.2 billion people—or 16 percent of the global population—do not have access to electricity, according to the International Energy Agency.

Alessandro Graf Volta.

■ *In 1800, the Italian scientist Alessandro Volta created the first electric cell, and the study of electricity really took off.*

electricians agree that this career offers a constantly-changing and rewarding work environment that allows them to make a difference in the world.

■ *An electrician at a job site discusses his job duties, necessary skills, and work environment.*

Construction Electricians

If you walk or drive by a construction site, there is probably at least one electrician at work installing wiring, troubleshooting newly installed electrical systems, and ensuring that all wiring and electrical systems and components are up to code. *Construction electricians* play an important role in the construction of homes, apartment buildings, businesses, factories, and other structures. They plan the layout and installation of electrical wiring, equipment, fixtures, and systems based on blue-prints created by architects, the **National Electrical Code**, and local building codes. According to O*NET OnLine, major duties of construction inspectors include:

- Assembling, installing, testing, and maintaining electronic and electrical wiring, hardware, equipment, and fixtures

- Using testing equipment to troubleshoot malfunctioning systems, components, and apparatus

- Connecting wires to **electrical conduits, circuit breakers,** transformers, and other components

- Inspecting completed electrical systems and equipment to identify potential hazards or set-up errors, and repairing or adjusting, as appropriate

If you enjoy building things from scratch, working as a member of a team, and having a diverse range of job duties, you'll like working as a construction electrician. Additionally, you'll need to be willing to work outdoors and in unheated homes under construction, which can be taxing on very hot or cold days. Travel to job sites is required, so you'll need a driver's license and a trustworthy vehicle.

Maintenance Electricians

Electrical systems and components keep our computers running; our lights on; our offices and stores cool in the summer and warm in the winter; and our factories churning out shiny new cars, slabs of steel and other building materials, and countless other products. *Maintenance electricians,* sometimes called *inside elec-*

■ *A maintenance electrician at a factory checks circuitry to ensure that production will stay on schedule.*

tricians, service and maintain electrical systems, large motors, equipment, and control systems at factories that manufacture cars, steel, or chemicals. They also work at large companies, government offices, apartment or condominium complexes, shopping centers, and other large facilities. Their duties include installing wiring and electrical systems; regularly inspecting all electrical infrastructure; making necessary repairs and changing defective circuit breakers, fuses, switches, and wiring; and roviding advice to executives regarding the purchase of new or replacement ystems.

large factory employs a team of electricians to ensure that it runs properly and no roduction time is lost. At a small company or condominium complex, you might be a member of a two- or three-person team or even the only electrician on staff.

Maintenance electricians have work environments that range from loud and busy actory floors (these types of electricians wear earplugs and other special protective ear), to quiet, climate-controlled offices or residential buildings. Most work indoors, ut some outdoor work is required to install, maintain, and service lighting, security, r other electrical systems.

he sudden loss of electricity or faltering of an electrical component on a busy roduction line can result in considerable frustration, the loss of productivity, and he loss of thousands, or even millions, of dollars in profits. As a result, maintenance lectricians are required to work a variety of shifts—from the standard 9-to-5 Monday-riday shift to at night and on weekends. Nontraditional shifts can be stressful to your ersonal life with family and friends, although some electricians enjoy the nontradi-ional hours.

■ *Check out electricians working in a variety of jobs.*

Becoming a Boss

lectricians who have at least five years of experience and a reputation for doing uality work can be promoted to the position of *foreman.* In this career, you'll manage

■ *A foreman reviews blueprints at a construction site.*

a team of electricians as they install, maintain, and repair electrical and power systems. Major job responsibilities for foremen include:

- Ensuring that crews meet project deadlines
- Occasionally assisting electricians with the assembly, installation, maintenance and testing of electrical equipment and wiring systems
- Checking finished work to ensure that it meets applicable building codes and project specifications
- Meeting with construction managers during the project to ensure that the work is being completed on-budget, on-time, and meeting other project guidelines
- Assessing the work of apprentices as they do their jobs to ensure that their skills and electrical knowledge are improving

A foreman may have to travel to multiple construction sites to manage work teams. Night work, weekend work, or both is required for some projects.

They Were Electricians!?

The film director **Alfred Hitchcock** electrified audiences with award-winning movies such as *Rear Window*, *Vertigo*, and *Psycho*, but did you know that before achieving cinematic fame, he was an electrician? At age sixteen, he left school to work as an apprentice electrician at W. T. Henley Ltd., a telegraph cable company. Here are a few other well-known people who worked as electricians or who experimented significantly with electricity before becoming successful in another field:

■ *Lech Walesa was working as an electrician when he co-founded Solidarity, the USSR's first independent trade union. He later served as president of Poland.*

Benjamin Franklin is known as one of America's Founding Fathers, but his experiments with electricity—including flying kites in lightning storms to determine if lightning was electrical—led to the invention of the lightning rod. For his work, Franklin received the Copley Medal from The Royal Society of London for Improving Natural Knowledge in 1753 and in 1756.

Inventor and Nobel-Prize-winner **Alfred Einstein** briefly worked for his father's company that manufactured electrical equipment based on direct current.

Lech Wałesa was working as an electrician when he co-founded Solidarity, the USSR's first independent trade union. He won the Nobel Peace Prize in 1983, and served as president of Poland.

■ *An electrical contractor checks an outside outlet for a customer. Owning your own business ca* *be extremely rewarding.*

Starting Your Own Contracting Business

Do you like to be your own boss? If so, a career as an *electrical contractor* is a good choice. An electrical contractor is simply a skilled electrician who owns his or her business. Your contracting business may consist of just you, or your company may be so successful that you'll need to hire other electricians and office staff to assist customers. Owning your own electrical services firm is a popular career path for electricians. In fact, nearly 56 percent of electricians in the United States are **self-employed**, according to the U.S. Department of Labor. That's much higher than the average (10.1 percent) for people in all careers.

Electrical contractors provide services to businesses, nonprofit organizations, government agencies, and homeowners. A large number of electrical contractors consist of small one-person shops that offer services to homeowners. Electrical issues common to homes include frequent electrical surges or fluctuations in power dead electrical outlets, dryers failing to heat up and dry clothing, light switches or fixtures not working properly, circuit breakers tripping frequently, electrical shocks, c gh electrical bills. In new home construction or a remodeling project, a contractor ight install new outlets and wiring as needed, or provide advice on setting up elec- ical systems for a room addition or an entire new home.

ectrical contractors who provide specialized construction services can be further assified as *outside* or *line contractors*, who ensure that high-voltage power is ansmitted safely through high-voltage power lines and substations to homes and usinesses; *inside contractors,* who handle electrical cabling design, installation, d maintenance in businesses, schools, condos, homes, and other buildings; *voice/ ata/video electrical contractors,* who work mainly with wireless networks, energy-ef- cient lighting, fiber optics, security systems, climate controls, and other low-voltage stallations and repairs; and *integrated building systems electrical contractors,* ho assess and network these systems to improve energy efficiency and overall erformance.

eing an electrical contractor is rewarding because you get to be your own boss, set ur own work schedule, and have the chance to receive much-higher earnings than salaried electrician if your business is successful. On the other hand, owning your wn business can be stressful and challenging. It's up to you to attract customers a word-of-mouth, newspaper ads, and even social media. You'll be responsible for lling customers and tracking down those who don't pay their bills. You'll also need manage staff and handle any other issues that arise. In short, the buck stops with u and you must be ready to work very hard to build a successful business.

elated Career Paths

ectricians who complete additional education and training are qualified to work in any related fields. Here are a few popular options:

ectric power-line technicians install, maintain, and fix power lines that transmit ectricity. They are employed by utilities and construction contractors.

elecommunications line technicians install, maintain, and repair telecommunica- ons cable, including fiber optic line. They may also install and maintain telecommu- ications equipment. Typical employers include telecommunication companies and nstruction contractors.

olar **photovoltaic** *installers* build, install, and maintain solar panel systems. Some nnect the solar arrays to the electric grid. They are employed by photovoltaic panel manufacturers; plumbing, heating, and air-conditioning contractors; electrical contractors and other wiring installation contractors; and power and communication line and related structures construction firms.

Wind turbine technicians install, maintain, and fix wind turbines, including their electrical, mechanical, and hydraulic components and systems. They work for wind turbine manufacturers; electric power generation, transmission, and distribution companies; and utility system construction firms.

Electric vehicle technicians (EVTs) install and repair charging stations and other equipment needed for electric vehicles. They assist engineers in the design and development of electrical components in electric or hybrid vehicles. EVTs are employed by electric car manufacturers and traditional car makers who also manufacture

■ *Electric power-line technicians must be willing to work at great heights to install and service electric power lines.*

ectric vehicles (such as Tesla, Renault-Nissan, Mitsubishi, Volkswagen, Ford, and eneral Motors), engineering firms that provide services to these manufacturers, and overnment agencies (such as the U.S. Department of Energy) that conduct research the field.

lectrical and electronics engineering technicians help engineers develop a variety of echnology such as tablet computers, communications equipment, security systems, edical imaging devices, automobile electrical systems, and airplane navigation rstems. They work in many industries—ranging from automotive and aerospace, to efense and medical devices, to telecommunications and computer hardware.

■ *Three experienced electricians talk about the rewards of becoming an electrician.*

taying Safe on the Job

lectricity is a powerful, but dangerous, force, and electricians must be extremely areful in their work to avoid serious injury or even death. Examples of accidents n the job include electrocution due to improperly installed wiring or miscommuni-ation regarding turned off power, flash burns from electrical explosions, repetitive novement injuries, exposure to lead solder and asbestos, and falls from ladders r other high places. To avoid injuries, and even death, electricians follow many afety practices. They wear protective clothing, including heavy gloves, steel-toed ork shoes, and sometimes eye goggles. They also use safety equipment such as ardhats, hearing protection, face shields, and body harnesses. Here are a few safety neasures to keep in mind if you work as an electrician:

■ *Electricians must wear heavy gloves and other protective gear to stay safe on the job.*

- When working on electrical equipment and circuit breakers, be sure the power turned off. This seems obvious, but thousands of people are injured each year after failing to take this important step before starting their work.

- Don't take electricity for granted—even if you have tons of experience. Check and double check yourself as you go about your work—especially when working with high voltage.

- Get your own equipment inspected to ensure that it is not damaged nor malfunctioning. Faulty equipment will put you in danger as you work.

- When possible, work with a second electrician or an apprentice or helper to ensure you'll get help quickly if you are electrocuted or suffer another serious injury.

Text-Dependent Questions

What type of electrician career(s) are a good fit if you enjoy building things from scratch or maintaining already-built equipment?

What are some challenging aspects of a career as an electrical contractor?

What kinds of safety gear do electricians use to protect themselves on the job?

Research Project

hat do you get when you combine two D batteries, a cardboard paper towel tube, a volt flashlight bulb, two brass fasteners, a small piece of cardboard, a paper clip, elec-cal tape, a bathroom-size paper cup, and number 22 insulated copper bell wire? A pile junk is not the answer! But if your answer was a "flashlight," you're correct. Visit http://ww.energizer.com/science-center/how-to-make-a-flashlight to learn how to build a flash-ght that is similar to the first flashlight ever created, which was developed by the inventor onrad Hubert in the 1890s.

CHAPTER 2

Tools of the Trade

Hand and Power Tools

conduit bender: A tool that bends conduit (a tube that is used to protect and direct electrical wiring) so that it can be fitted into various types of spaces during the installation process. Available as a simple hand bender, as well as in mechanical, electric, and hydraulic models.

drill: A hand or power tool that is fitted with a cutting tool attachment or driving tool attachment; it is used to cut into material ranging from wood and stone, to metal and plastic.

hand saw: A cutting tool with a long, thin serrated steel blade; it is operated using a backward and forward movement.

pliers: A hand tool that is used to hold objects firmly, as well as bend and compress a variety of materials.

power saw: A cutting device that is battery- or electric-powered.

screwdriver: A manual or powered device that turns screws; available with a flattened, cross-shaped style (known as a flathead screwdriver), or with a star-shaped tip that fits into the head of a screw to turn it (often referred to as a Phillips® screwdriver).

wire crimper: A hand tool that joins two pieces of metal or other ductile material (typically a wire and a metal plate).

wire stripper: A hand-held tool that is used to remove insulation from electric wires.

Measuring Tools

laser measure: A device that allows users to take distance measurements instantly.

level: A device that is used to establish a horizontal plane. It is comprised of a small glass tube that contains alcohol or a similar liquid and an air bubble.

tape measure: A flexible ruler made up of fiber glass, a metal strip, cloth, or plastic.

Troubleshooting Tools

ammeter: An instrument that measures the current in a circuit.

thermal imaging scanner: A device used by electricians, home inspectors, and others to identify basic electrical connection and load problems, find moisture intrusion, detect energy loss/missing insulation, and perform other functions.

voltmeter: An instrument that is used to measure the potential difference, or voltage, between two points in an electrical or electronic circuit. Also known as a **voltage meter.**

Computer Technology

building information modeling software: A computer application that uses a 3D model-based process that helps construction, architecture, and engineering professionals to more efficiently plan, design, build, and manage buildings and infrastructure.

office management software: A computer application that helps users track finances and manage billing, draft correspondence, and perform other tasks.

CHAPTER 3

Terms of the Trade

alternating current: An electric charge that changes direction periodically. Used to deliver power to houses and office buildings.

battery: A collection of two or more power sources in which chemical energy is converted into electricity. The battery is used as a source of power.

capacitance: The ability of a battery or system to store a charge. Measured in farads.

circuit breaker: A device in a building or structure that stops the flow of excess current that may damage the electrical circuit.

conductor: Copper wires with no insulation that serve as the path through which electricity flows in an electrical circuit.

conduit-bending: The process of bending conduit (a tube that is used to protect and direct electrical wiring) so that it can be fitted into various types of spaces during the installation process. A conduit bender can consist of a simple hand bender, as well as mechanical, electric, and hydraulic models.

conduit: A tube that is used to protect and direct electrical wiring in a building or structure. Conduit may be made of metal, fiber, plastic, or fired clay.

current: A measure of electrical flow. It is measured in amperes.

direct current: An electric charge that only travels in one direction. Devices that plug in to the wall with an AC adapter, are powered by a battery, or use a USB cable for power rely on direct current.

electrical charge: A unit of positive and negative energy (commonly carried by protons and electrons respectively). Measured in coulombs.

lectrical circuit: A line or path through which an electrical current flows. An electrical circuit must be closed (joined at both nds) to make the flow of current possible. A basic electrical rcuit consists of conductors, a switch, a load, and a power urce (also known as a cell).

lectrical conduit: A tube that is used to protect and direct lectrical wiring. It is made of metal, plastic, fiber, or fired clay.

lectrical current: A flow of electrical charge that is measured amperes.

oad: In an electrical circuit, a small buzzer or light bulb that uzzes or lights when the circuit is turned on. Also known as a esistor.

ational Electrical Code: A series of rules in the United States r safe electrical design, installation, and inspection that were eveloped by the National Fire Protection Association. The code as been adopted in all 50 states.

rogrammable logic controller: An industrial computer nat is designed to operate in demanding conditions (extreme emperatures, wet or dusty conditions, etc.) to control manufacuring processes.

esistance: The measure of opposition to the flow of electricity. is measured in ohms.

chematic diagram: An illustration of the components of a ystem that uses abstract, graphic symbols instead of realistic ictures or illustrations.

witch: A small gap in the conductor where one can close (elecicity flows) or open (electricity does not flow) a circuit.

ransformer: A device that conveys electrical energy from one ircuit to another without any direct electrical connection.

■ *Participating in an apprenticeship is the most-popular way to train to become an electrician.*

Words to Understand

apprenticeship: A formal training program that combines classroom instruction and supervised practical experience. Apprentices are paid a salary that increases as they obtain experience.

community college: A private or public two-year college that awards certificates and associate degrees.

professional network: Friends, family, coworkers, former teachers, and others who can help you find a job.

technical college: A public or private college that offers two- or four-year programs in practical subjects, such as the trades, information technology, applied sciences, agriculture, and engineering.

union: An organization that seeks to gain better wages, benefits, and working conditions for its members. Also called a **labor union** or **trade union**.

CHAPTER 4

Preparing for the Field and Making a Living

Educational Paths

You love tinkering with electronics—building a flashlight from scratch, creating a simple circuit, etc.—but how do you turn that interest into a career as an electrician? Young people who want to become electricians can pursue several educational paths: participate in an apprenticeship (the most popular entry method), attend a technical school or community college, learn through informal methods such as working as a helper with an experienced electrician, or receive training in the military. All these paths are viable ways to enter this career, but no matter what path you pursue, you'll need to work extremely hard to achieve your goals.

■ *High school shop students learn about electrical concepts.*

High School Classes

Before you start your formal training, you should obtain experience working with electricity and tools, as well as the larger mathematical concepts involved in the generation and transmission of electricity. That way, you'll be prepared to excel in your apprenticeship or other educational path. Several

■ *An instructor teaches two apprentices how to use a voltmeter.*

classes will help you hone your technical, mathematical, and other skills necessary to be a successful electrician. For example, shop classes will teach you how to use tools, build basic electrical components and systems, troubleshoot problems as you construct things, and learn many other skills. Some schools even offer specialized curricula in electricity. For example, McCann Technical High School in Massachusetts has an Electricity Program Curriculum that "takes a student from the simple low voltage circuit through residential, commercial, and industrial wiring up to and including complex motor control circuits. All phases of proper wiring methods are taught in both shop and theory classes." In this program, students learn about motors, generators, controllers, transformers, programmable logic controllers, and fire and security alarm circuits.

Even if your school doesn't have an extensive program like McCann's, shop classes will teach you the ins and outs of conduit bending, load assessment, blueprint reading, and other skills.

lectricians must know how to add, subtract, multiply, divide, compute fractions and ercentages, and calculate various things like voltage drop, conduit shrinkage, and ending angles, so be sure to take math classes, including basic algebra and trigo- ometry.

omputer science classes are important because electricians increasingly work buildings that are run by complex systems that use computer processors, fiber ptics, sophisticated controls, and networking equipment. Electrical contractors also se computers, apps, and other technology for everything from tracking customer ppointments and record keeping, to accounting and marketing.

you plan to start your own company, be sure to take business, marketing, English/ riting, and accounting classes. A foreign language such as Spanish will come handy if you work in areas where many people do not speak English as a first anguage.

■ *View interviews with several apprentices and learn about classroom and hands-on requirements for apprentices.*

pprenticeships

1ost electricians prepare for the field by completing an apprenticeship program, /hich typically lasts four to five years, although some programs are shorter. During ach year in the program, trainees complete 2,000 hours of on-the-job training and .44 hours of related classroom instruction.

pprenticeship programs are offered by the International Brotherhood of Electrical /orkers (IBEW) and National Electrical Contractors Association (NECA), via local ffiliate programs that use curricula created by the Electrical Training Alliance;

■ *An apprentice receives hands-on training at a job site.*

Associated Builders and Contractors; and Independent Electrical Contractors. Entry requirements vary by program, but here are typical requirements for those applying to an IBEW/NECA Joint Apprenticeship Training Program or an IBEW/NECA Area Wide Joint Apprenticeship Program:

- Minimum age of eighteen
- High school education
- One year of high school algebra
- Qualifying score on an aptitude test
- Drug free

ccording to Independent Electrical Contractors, general electrical apprentices ceive instruction in electrical skills; electrical theory; codes and standards; resi- ntial, commercial, and industrial wiring; fire alarm, signaling, and life safety stems; lighting systems; transformers; motors and control; electrical trouble- ooting; mechanical skills; and safety, first aid, and CPR. Those seeking to specialize residential electrical service also learn about residential wiring; residential lighting stems; and residential fire alarm, signaling, and life safety systems. Those special- ing in data-telecommunications learn about data and telecommunications cabling;

Electrician Career Path

If you work hard, there are great opportunities for advancement in the electrical trades. Here is a typical career ladder for electricians.

Business Owner: Operates an electrical contracting firm that provides services to homeowners and businesses.

Project Manager: Oversees the electrical work for entire projects. Is responsible for staffing, ordering supplies and equipment, quality control, and other tasks.

Master Electrician: Has either seven years of work experience as a licensed electrician or a bachelor's degree in electrical engineering and must pass an examination. Manages journeymen electricians and apprentices.

Foreman: A journeyman electrician who manages a group of other journeymen and apprentices on a project.

Journeyman Electrician: Has completed apprenticeship training. If licensed, can work by him- or herself without direct supervision, but, for large projects, must work under permits issued to a master electrician.

Apprentice Electrician: Apprentice electricians in the U.S. complete 2,000 hours of on-the-job training and 144 hours of related classroom instruction during a four- to five-year course of study.

copper and fiber-optic connections and splices; audio and video systems; life safety systems; security systems; wireless communications; and building automation.

If you live in the U.S., visit www.doleta.gov/OA/sainformation.cfm for information on apprenticeship training programs in your state.

As they progress in the program, apprentices expand their skill sets, take on more responsibility, and receive higher wages. Those who complete an electrical apprenticeship training program are known as *journeymen electricians.* Most U.S. states

■ *A project manager reviews electrical schematics at a construction site.*

require that electricians become licensed; the requirements vary by state.

Journeymen electricians who have either seven years of work experience as licensed electricians or a bachelor's degree in electrical engineering *and* pass an examination can become *master electricians.*

Technical and Community College

Some aspiring electricians choose to prepare for the field by earning a certificate and/or an associate of applied science in electrical/electronic engineering technology or a related field from a **technical college** or **community college**. They als otain practical experience by completing an internship or informal apprenticeship ith a construction firm or other company that employs electricians. It's a good ea to attend a program that has been accredited by the Technology Accreditation ommission of the Accreditation Board for Engineering and Technology. This organiation accredits schools in the United States and twenty-five other countries. Other ations have their own accrediting bodies.

nformal Training Opportunities

an informal training opportunity, you will work for three to five years as an elecician helper at a construction site or for an electrical contractor. Gradually, you'll ain the skills and experience (combined with some formal training at a technical chool) to pursue licensing as an electrician. This type of entry method was much ore popular several decades ago, but some aspiring electricians still prepare for is career using this method.

ilitary

ne military needs electricians to keep the power running at hospitals, airplane angars, and other facilities; install wiring in buildings under construction; and oubleshoot electrical problems. The U.S. Army, Marines, and Navy, as well as many

A Navy electrician inspects fuse boxes in the forward pump room of an aircraft carrier.

militaries in other countries, provide training for electricians. According to TodaysMil-
itary.com, job training in the U.S. military branches "consists of classroom instruction
including practice in the installation and repair of electrical wiring systems. Further
training occurs on the job and through advanced courses." The military is an excellent
way to receive training tuition free, but keep in mind that it offers no guarantee that
you'll receive your first choice for a career. It gets the final say on where it needs your
services. So, even if you want to be an electrician, you might end up peeling potatoes
as a navy cook or on the front lines as an army infantry person in a war zone.

Other Training Opportunities

Some electrical contractors operate their own training programs. While they are not
recognized apprenticeship programs, they provide similar classroom and on-the-job
instruction. Check with contractors in your area regarding potential training opportunities.

■ *An informal training opportunity is a good choice for those who want to get to work right away as
an electrician helper.*

Salaries for Electricians by U.S. State

Earnings for electricians vary widely by state based on demand and other factors. Here are the five states where employers pay the highest average salary and the states in which employers pay the lowest salaries.

Highest Average Salaries:

- Alaska: $81,600
- Hawaii: $74,770
- Illinois: $73,160
- New York: $73,010
- New Jersey: $71,310

Source: U.S. Department of Labor

Lowest Average Salaries:

- Arkansas: $42,540
- North Carolina: $42,960
- South Carolina: $43,560
- Florida: $44,310
- Alabama: $46,360

ome electricians enter apprenticeship programs after first working as a helper. The lome Builders Institute (HBI) offers a preapprenticeship certificate training program or electricians. The program was created to serve diverse populations such as transioning military members, secondary and postsecondary students, veterans, unemloyed and displaced workers, and justice-involved youth and adults. In the program, articipants learn how to install electrical conduit and wiring, circuit panels, switches, eceptacles, and lighting fixtures for homes and commercial sites; how to conduct ystems testing and repair; and how to use green construction techniques to reduce esources and conserve energy. In some areas, students also learn how to install and naintain solar systems. In addition to offering training in the electrical trades, HBI rovides programs in carpentry, plumbing, landscaping, masonry, painting, building onstruction technology, and weatherization.

■ *Watch an apprentice at work and learn about the strong salaries and steady demand for electricians.*

Which Educational Path is Best for Me?

There are several ways to prepare to become an electrician. Each has its pros and cons.

Apprenticeships are the most popular preparation method because they provide a clear path to employment. Once you successfully complete your apprenticeship, the company that employed you may offer you a job. And what's not to like about that? And if you do not get an offer and need to search for a job, the fact that you completed an apprenticeship will impress hiring managers and help you get the new position. Although the apprenticeship road is long (four to five years), the rewards are great: good salary, a high probability of a job, strong industry contacts, and a great credential on your resume. An apprenticeship program is a good path for those who like a structured environment that combines both classroom and hands-on training. It is also a good fit for those who are patient and willing to commit to a four- or five-year training program.

Training to become an electrician at a technical school or community college involves a similar educational structure to that of an apprenticeship, but these programs are typically two to three years shorter than apprenticeship programs. This type of training is a good fit for those who want to enter the workforce more quickly, although graduates have no assurance of a job once they graduate.

An informal training opportunity is a good choice for those who want to get to work ght away as an electrician helper. Those who do not need a structured educational etting to learn, who are able to pick up their skills and knowledge on the job, and vho are flexible regarding work duties will prosper in this training path.

Military training involves both classroom and hands-on training. Those who respect authority, can follow instructions, have a disciplined personality, and who are willing o make a commitment to serve their country for two or more years are a good match or this training method.

Networking is an excellent way to land a job as an electrician. Teachers, apprenticeship coordinators, and former classmates can be good sources of job leads.

Getting a Job

You've completed your training to become an electrician. Now what? You may already ave received a job offer, but, if not, you'll have to look for a job. Here are some ommon job-search methods for job seekers:

Use Your Network. During your training, you've hopefully gotten to know some of our classmates, instructors, job foremen, and others. Reach out to this **professional network** to learn about job opportunities. Perhaps one of your classmates ust landed a job on a new construction project that is in dire need of more electricians. Or you could mention to one of your favorite instructors that you're looking for a job. He or she has many industry contacts, and may be able to direct you to companies that are hiring. Be sure to see if your family and friends are aware of new construction projects or other positions for electricians. Don't forget to use social networking sites such as LinkedIn to network, learn about potential employers, talk "shop" with other electricians, and even apply for a job. The key is to tell as many people as possible that you're looking for a job.

Check Out Job Boards. Some electricians learn about new jobs by checking out internet job boards that allow users to search by geographic region, salary, job type, employer name, and other criteria. Here are a few popular job boards:

- https://www.indeed.com/q-Electrician-jobs.html
- https://www.monster.com/jobs/q-electrician-jobs.aspx
- http://www.glassdoor.com
- https://www.usajobs.gov (U.S. federal government job board)

Join and Use the Resources of Unions and Professional Associations. About 33 percent of all electricians in the United States belong to a **union**. The main union for electricians is the International Brotherhood of Electrical Workers (IBEW). Other unions for electricians include the International Union of Electronic, Electrical, Salaried, Machine, and Furniture Workers; the International Association of Machinists and Aerospace Workers; the International Union, United Automobile, Aircraft and Agricultural Implement Workers of America; and the United Steelworkers of America.

There are many benefits to union membership. Electricians who are members of the IBEW and other unions typically receive higher earnings, better benefits, and more job security than those who are not members of unions. Additionally, once you are a member of a union, you'll have access to a large network of people who can give you tips on landing a job or even direct you to job openings. Some unions, such as the IBEW (http://www.ibew.org/Tools/Construction-Jobs-Board), have job boards, where you can look for jobs.

Be sure to also check out the resources provided by professional associations, which offer membership, training opportunities, networking events, and certification. Most countries have at least one professional association for electricians or electrical contractors. For example, major organizations in the United States include Independent Electrical Contractors and the National Electrical Contractors Association.

e Canadian Electrical Contractors Association represents the interests of more
an 8,000 electrical contractors across Canada. The Electrical Contractors' Asso-
ation is a major trade association for companies involved in electrical projects in
gland, Northern Ireland, and Wales. And organizations such as the International
ciety of Certified Electronic Technicians provide certification programs. Those who
e certified typically earn higher salaries and have better job prospects than those
o are not certified.

ow Much Can I Earn?

r all the talk of how a college degree is the ticket to a well-paying stable career, it's
come increasingly clear in recent years that skilled trades workers such as elec-
ians can earn incomes that are comparable, and sometimes even higher, than
se with degrees. And, unlike college students, apprentices begin earning as soon
they begin learning and often don't incur education-related debt. (The average U.S.
lege undergraduate has $37,172 in student loan debt, according to The Institute
College Access & Success. And The College Board reports that 11 percent of

Electrical contractors with thriving businesses can earn $120,000 to $200,000 or more a year.

graduate degree recipients have $120,000 or more in student debt.) Apprentices typically begin by earning between 40 percent and 50 percent of what trained electricians make, and receive pay increases as they gain experience. The U.S. Department of Labor reports that the average starting salary for apprentices is $60,000.

Average Earnings

Average annual salaries for all electricians are $56,650, according to the U.S. Department of Labor (USDL). The average pay for all workers in the U.S. is $49,630. Ten percent of electricians (typically those without much experience) earn $31,800 year.

The USDL reports the following average annual earnings for electricians by employe

- local government, $65,330;
- utility system construction, $61,250;
- building equipment contractors, $55,730;
- nonresidential building construction, $55,170;
- ship and boat building, $51,920.

Electrician helpers earn median salaries of $29,530, according to the USDL. Ten percent of helpers earn less than $20,110, while 10 percent earn $44,450 or more

Top Earners

The top 10 percent of electricians make $90,420 or more, according to the USDL. Who makes this type of money? The most-experienced, highly-skilled electricians; those with supervisory or managerial duties; and those who live in large cities and other areas with high demand for electricians and a shortage of workers. Electrical contractors with thriving businesses can earn $120,000 to $200,000 or more, depending on the size of their companies.

Union members often receive medical insurance, a pension, and other benefits from their union. Self-employed workers must provide their own fringe benefits.

Text-Dependent Questions

What high school classes should you take to prepare for training to become an electrician?

What is the most popular training method for aspiring electricians, and how long does this training last?

How much can electrical contractors earn?

Research Project

earn more about apprenticeships by visiting https://www.dol.gov/apprenticeship nd http://www.exploreapprenticeship.wa.gov/what.htm. Ask your shop teacher r school counselor to help set up an informational interview with an electrical pprentice or apprenticeship coordinator to expand your knowledge of the appren-ceship process.

ON THE JOB

Interview with a Professional

Randall Tyle is the coordinator of the Inside Electrician Apprenticeship Program at Lane Community College (LCC) in Eugene, Oregon, and the owner of Apprenticeship Training Services.

Q. Can you tell me a little about the inside electrician apprenticeship program at LCC? Is there anything that surprises new apprentices about the program?

A. The program at LCC is run by a private nonprofit trade association (Independent Electrical Contractors, Mid-Oregon Chapter). It is a four-year training program involving mostly on-the-job (OJT) training and related classroom instruction. Apprentices are employed with registered training agents (contractors) who provide the OJT portion of the training and are certified by the program to conduct that training. Students registered in this program receive both trades training and college credits simultaneously. Most apprentices have enough college credits upon completion to earn an AAS degree, by taking a few general education classes (math, writing, and science). The thing that surprises most applicants for the program is just how competitive these positions are. Most recent high school graduates are not very competitive. Things that make you more competitive are:

- A high school diploma is worth more than a GED on the application
- Knowledge of CPR/first aid
- Work history (especially involving construction)
- Good driving record; two or more moving violations under age twenty-five usually keeps a person from a job
- Types of classes and grades from high school; we generally value more advanced math and science classes
- Shop or industrial arts classes
- Experience with drafting or computer-aided design

Q. What are the benefits of training via an apprenticeship as opposed to other training methods?

A. Apprenticeship is the ONLY method available to obtain a license in those trades requiring licensure. I get a lot of post-college grads (10 percent four-year degree/20 percent two-year degree) who only figured this out after attending college. Additionally, there are multiple reasons that an apprenticeship is a better avenue for someone who likes working with their hands at a variety of jobsites, where the job changes daily or even hourly. The BIGGEST benefi that not only are you getting the training you need to become licensed, but you are also working in that field and getting paid. Wages start at $13 to $14 per hour and students in year four make $25 to $29 per hour. Also, the tuition cost for the classes is minimal and is often times either paid for outright by the employer or reimbursed upon completion of the classes.

. What kind of personal traits are important for electricians?

. The things I hear most from employers have little to do with the actual work itself. We can train someone to become an electrician. However, we cannot train them to be a good employee. Important traits include: being on time; asking good questions; working without being told to work or what to do; no cell phone use on the job (your Facebook updates can wait!); and good attendance. Additionally, applicants for the trades (specifically electrician) should have a strong understanding of algebra and physics. They should have a basic understanding of craft tools and basic carpentry, understand how to read or even draw blueprints, should not be afraid of heights or confined spaces, and should be in good physical condition.

. What are the pros and cons of being an electrician?

. Pros

- Great pay and benefits (average wages post-apprenticeship range from $35–$50 per hour)
- Changing work assignments and locations
- High-demand jobs; currently there is a shortage of trained electricians across the United States
- Cannot be outsourced
- Work where you actually get to build/make things
- Being a part of a team

ons

- Work can often times be physically challenging
- Loud, hazardous construction sites
- Industrial facilities
- Have to work in crawl spaces and attics in residential settings
- Construction jobs can (at times) be affected by the economy
- Some companies require travel (in state or even out of state)
- Electricity is dangerous and sometimes deadly

. What advice would you give to a young person who is considering a career as n electrician?

. Really decide that it is what you want to do/become. Like the advice I give to ANY student I talk with, actually spend some time with an electrician or electrical contractor and job shadow. earn what the day-to-day life is like for someone in that occupation. Be patient and persistent it is truly your calling. I have had applicants wait as long as four years for an opening in the rogram.

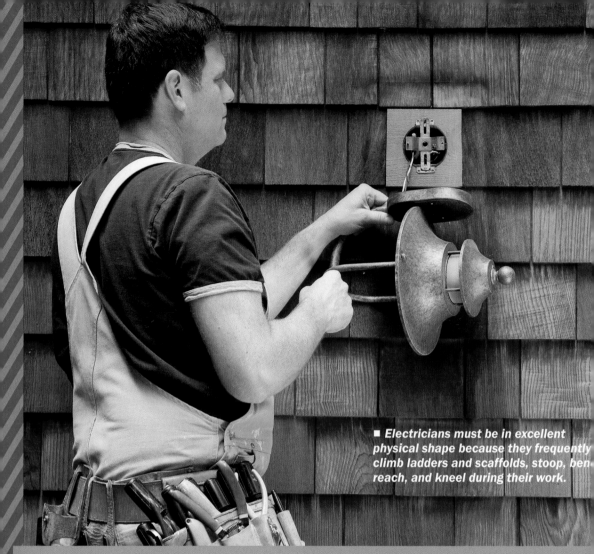

■ *Electricians must be in excellent physical shape because they frequently climb ladders and scaffolds, stoop, bend, reach, and kneel during their work.*

Words to Understand

conduit-bending: The process of bending conduit (a tube that is used to protect and direct electrical wiring) so that it can be fitted into various types of spaces during the installation process. A conduit bender can consist of a simple hand bender, as well as mechanical, electric, and hydraulic models.

schematic diagram: An illustration of the components of a system that uses abstract, graphic symbols instead of realistic pictures or illustrations.

soldering: The process of joining two metal items by using a material called solder, which melts when placed on a hot object.

CHAPTER 5

Key Skills and Methods of Exploration

What All Electricians Need

Some people who become electricians think that all you need for success is a mastery of the ins and outs of electrical wiring, components, and systems. But there's much more to being an electrician than knowing electrical theory and installation techniques. Here are some key personal skills and physical traits for electricians:

- **Color vision.** You must be able to identify electrical wires by color. If you are unable to identify wiring by color, you risk injury or even death.

- **Physical stamina and strength.** You'll spend a great deal of your day climbing ladders or scaffolds, standing, stooping, bending, reaching, kneeling, and bending. You

■ *Electrical contractors need strong customer service and communication skills because they frequently work with the public.*

may have to move heavy parts and equipment that can weigh more than 50 pounds. Other important physical traits include good manual dexterity, eye-hand coordination, and balance.

- **Troubleshooting and critical-thinking skills.** Much of your job—even if you work in new construction—consists of finding, diagnosing, and repairing problems. You need to have good brain power (or "wattage," to use an electric pun) to identify where a problem is occurring and the most time- and cost-effective steps to fix the issue.
- **Patience.** Troubleshooting takes time, and sometimes your best efforts fail to initially fix the problem. In this case, you must be patient and levelheaded to "stick-with-it" to identify and fix the problem.

Facts About Electricity

Electricity travels at the speed of light. This is more than 186,000 miles per second.

A bolt of lightning can measure up to three million volts.

Electricity can be generated from coal, wind, the sun, water, oil, nuclear power, natural gas, and even animal poop.

■ *A bolt of lightning can measure up to three million volts.*

Natural gas provides 33.8 percent of electricity in the United States. Coal supplies 30.4 percent; nuclear energy, 19.7 percent; hydropower, 6.5 percent; wind, 5.6 percent; other renewable resources, such as solar and geothermal, 2.8 percent; and fuel oil, 0.6 percent.

In the United States, total electric power industry capability is forecast to increase by 20 percent from 2017 through 2040. Demand for electricity is expected to grow by 19 percent during this same time span.

Sources: Alliant Energy, U.S. Department of Energy, Edison Electric Institute, Energy Information Administration

- **Teamwork/interpersonal/communication skills.** If you work as a member of a team, you'll need to learn how to work with people from all different backgrounds, ethnicities, and experience levels.

- **Ability to work independently.** At times, you may be the only electrician on site. In this instance, you need to be able to follow instructions without supervision and manage your time efficiently.

- **Customer-service skills.** If you work as a residential electrical contractor, you'll interact with people daily. There's a lot of competition out there, and only those contractors who are friendly, willing to take the time to answer customers' questions and concerns in a respectful manner, and otherwise provide top-quality customer service will have thriving businesses.

- **Business skills.** If you're self-employed, you must be skilled at marketing your business, bidding on jobs, overseeing staff, planning payroll, scheduling work appointments, and performing other tasks that keep your company running smoothly.

Exploring Electricity as a Student

As a middle school or high school student it may seem like it's difficult to explore electricity and the career of electrician, but this couldn't be further from the truth. There are countless ways—such as classes, clubs, and competitions, to do-it-yourself activities, and information interviews—to learn more. Here are some popular methods of exploration:

■ *Get some hands-on experience by learning how to measure voltage.*

■ *Students in an electronics club discuss a project with their teacher.*

Take Some Classes. Several classes will help you to learn more about electricity and prepare for a career in the field. In shop class, for example, you'll learn about electrical theory, structural blueprint reading, construction principles, safety practices, and much more. Some schools offer specialized curricula in electricity in their shop classes. In such a program, you might troubleshoot electrically-controlled equipment; study single-phase and three-phase transformation by utilizing programmable logic controllers; and learn how to assess and use wiring and **schematics diagrams**. Other useful classes include math (particularly basic algebra and trigonometry), computer science; and business, marketing, English/writing, and accounting classes (if you plan to start your own company).

Join or Start an Electronics Club at Your School. In such a club, you'll learn about electricity, electronics, technology, and engineering, as well as participate in competitions to build electronic circuits, mini electric vehicles, and other electrical-related projects. Your faculty advisor may be able to organize presentations by electri-

ians or electrical/electronics engineers or tours of construction sites or manufacturing plants. If your school doesn't have an electronics club, ask your shop teacher
for help in forming one. Or start your own with a group of like-minded friends.

Join the Technology Student Association. If you're a middle school or high school
student and interested in science, technology, engineering, and mathematics (STEM),
consider joining the Technology Student Association (TSA, http://www.tsaweb.org).
This national, nonprofit organization offers sixty competitions at its annual conference,
as well as opportunities to develop your leadership skills, perform community service,
and compete for money for college. Ask your school counselor or science teacher if
your school has a TSA chapter and, if not, encourage them to start one.

Participate in a Competition. Competing in a contest is a good way to build your
skills, make new friends, and test your abilities against those of your classmates or
students from around the country or world. Competitions are sponsored by schools,

Participating in electronics competitions is an excellent way to explore the field.

local park districts, technology companies, or regional, national, or international membership organizations for young people interested in STEM. Here are two well-known organizations that host competitions that will allow you to develop and demonstrate your electrical skills and knowledge:

- **SkillsUSA** (http://www.skillsusa.org) is a "national membership organization serving middle-school, high-school, and college/postsecondary students who are preparing for careers in trade, technical, and skilled service occupations." Its SkillsUSA Championships involve competitions in one-hundred events. Students first compete locally, with winners advancing to state and national levels. A small number of winners can even advance to compete against young people from more than seventy-five other countries at WorldSkills International, which was recently held in Abu Dhabi, United Arab Emirates, and in Leipzig, Germany. SkillsUSA offers several electricity-related competitions. For example, in the Electrical Construction Wiring Competition, students must complete a written test that assesses their knowledge of the National Electric Code; a practical conduit-bending exercise and hands-on installation of a conduit system, cabling system, and wiring devices; and assess drawings and specification sheets to install an electrical system that is common in residential and light commercial projects. In the Electronics Technology Competition, participants must demonstrate their mastery of customer service, the design and selection of circuit components, soldering, troubleshooting electronic circuits, and knowledge of proper safety practices, among other skills. Other competitions are available in Industrial Motor Control, Internetworking, Mechatronics, Mobile Electronics Installation, Mobile Robotics Technology, Power Equipment Technology, Related Technical Math, and Residential Systems Installation and Maintenance. SkillsUSA works directly with high schools and colleges, so ask your school counselor or teacher if it is an option for you.

- **The Technology Student Association** (http://www.tsaweb.org) a membership organization for middle and high school students interested in STEM, offers many competitions that allow students to demonstrate their skills. For example, middle school students can participate in the Electrical Applications Competition. First, they take a written test that assesses their knowledge of basic electrical and electronic theory. Then, semifinalists build a specific circuit from a schematic diagram using a provided kit, make required electrical measure-

One of the best ways to learn more about electricity is to build something. Above, a student ~~sh~~ows off a robotic arm that she is building.

ments, and explain their methods to the judges. In the Animatronics Competition, high school students "demonstrate knowledge of mechanical and control systems by designing, fabricating, and controlling an animatronics device that will communicate, entertain, inform, demonstrate and/or illustrate a topic, idea, subject, or concept. Sound, lights, and a surrounding environment must accompany the device." Other contests available for those with an interest in electricity and building things include TEAMS (Tests of Engineering Aptitude, Mathematics and Science), a one-day competition for students in middle and high school; Junior Solar Sprint, an educational program for fifth through eighth graders; and the VEX Robotics Competition for middle and high school students.

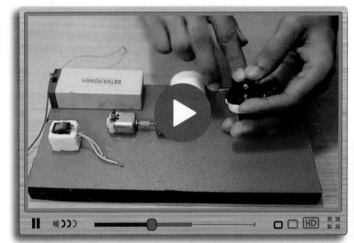

■ *Build a basic electrical generator at home.*

Build Something! One of the best ways to learn more about electricity is to actually build or repair something. For example, you might repair an old radio or computer or build an electrical kit. Ask your shop teacher to provide project ideas. YouTube is an excellent source of how-to videos. And the following books offer good project ideas:

- *20 Makey Makey Projects for the Evil Genius,* by Aaron Graves and Colleen Graves (McGraw-Hill Education, 2017).

- *Make: Design Your Own Circuits: 17 Exciting Design Ideas for New Electronics Projects,* by Charles Platt (Maker Media, Inc., 2018).

- *Safe and Simple Electrical Experiments,* 2nd ed., by Rudolf F. Graf (Maker Media, Inc., 2015).

our a Construction Site or Manufacturing Plant. Ask your school counselor
 shop teacher to arrange a tour of a construction site, factory, or other place
here electricians work. That way, you'll be able to see electricians at work and ask
em questions about their job duties, the tools they use, and other topics. Some
dustry organizations (such as Go Construct in the United Kingdom and Associated
onstruction Contractors of New Jersey in the United States) arrange tours to educate
oung people about construction specialties. You can also simply reach out to
onstruction associations in your area for information on tour opportunities.

alk to or Job Shadow an Electrician. One of the best ways to learn more about
is career is to participate in an information interview with an electrician. In such an
terview, you gather information, but do not seek a job. Many electricians are happy

Touring a construction site is a great way to learn about a career as an electrician.

to discuss their careers with young people. Here are some questions to ask during the interview:

- Can you tell me about a day in your life on the job?
- Do you have to travel for your job?

Sources of Additional Exploration

Contact the following organizations for more information on education and careers in electricity:

electrical training ALLIANCE

888-652-4007

www.electricaltrainingalliance.org

Independent Electrical Contractors

800-456-4324

info@ieci.org

www.ieci.org

International Brotherhood of Electrical Workers

202-833-7000

www.ibew.org

International Society of Certified Electronic Technicians

800-946-0201

info@iscet.org

www.iscet.org

National Electrical Contractors Association

301-657-3110

www.necanet.org

- What are the most important personal and professional qualities for people in your career?
- What do you like best and least about your job?
- What is the future employment outlook for electricians? How is the field changing?
- What can I do now to prepare for the field?

u might also be able to job shadow an electrician. This basically involves you lowing the electrician around for a few hours or even an entire day on the job. ere's no better way to learn about the job duties, tools, safety practices, and wards and challenges of being an electrician than observing one at work.

ur school counselor, unions and professional associations (such as the Interna- nal Brotherhood of Electrical Workers), and friends and family who know electri- ins can help you arrange an information interview or job shadowing experience. 1one of these sources pan out, try contacting an electrician on LinkedIn (https:// w.linkedin.com). You'll be surprised at how many people are willing to help you irn more about electrician careers.

lunteer and Learn. Volunteering with a local or other community group that ilds or repairs homes for senior citizens, those whose homes have been damaged natural disasters, and others who need a helping hand is a good way to learn the sics of electricity and watch an electrician at work. No, you won't be connecting res to conduits or circuit breakers, but you will be able to work as a helper. You'll ch wire and conduit, handle tools, and otherwise assist the electrician. One ganization to check out is Habitat for Humanity, which operates in nearly 1,400 mmunities across the U.S. and in more than seventy countries around the world to nstruct affordable housing and repair existing homes for those in need. Through Youth Programs (https://www.habitat.org/volunteer/near-you/youth-programs), bitat for Humanity offers volunteer opportunities for those age five to forty. High hool and college students can start a Habitat chapter at their schools, volunteer to ild or repair houses for a week during school breaks, and participate in other activ- 's that allow them to learn about home construction and make the world a better ice.

■ A high school student job shadows an electric foreman at a construction site.

Text-Dependent Questions

- Why is it important for an electrician to have good color vision?

- What is SkillsUSA and what does it offer to students?

- What is an information interview? What questions should you ask during such an interview?

Research Project

lectricians must be in good physical shape to be successful on the job. Learn more bout how to stay fit and healthy by visiting https://www.healthychildren.org/English/ ges-stages/teen/fitness/Pages/How-Teens-Can-Stay-Fit.aspx, http://www.safeteens. rg/nutrition-exercise/exercise-fitness, and https://www.hhs.gov/fitness/be-active/ ays-to-be-active/index.html. Set daily health and fitness goals for yourself and keep record of your progress.

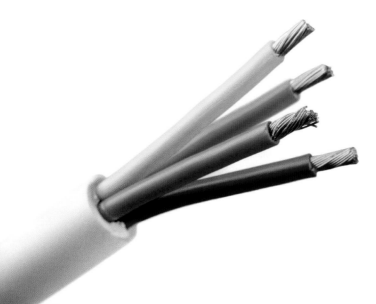

Words to Understand

artificial intelligence: The simulation of human intelligence by machinery and computer systems.

Great Recession: A period of significant economic decline worldwide, beginning in December 2007 and ending in June 2009, in which many banks failed, the real estate sector crashed, trade declined, and many people became unemployed.

smart home technology: Electronic systems that automatically control and monitor lighting, heating, ventilation, security systems, as well as appliances. They can be commanded by voice, remote control, tablet, or smartphone.

CHAPTER 6

The Future of the Electrician Occupation

The Big Picture

Access to electricity—to power our homes, air conditioners, smartphones, and electric vehicles—has become an expectation, not a luxury, in many countries. And this expectation ensures that there will always be strong demand for electricians. But despite a great need for electricians, there's a shortage of skilled workers in many countries. Why? Many Baby Boomers are retiring from these trades, and subsequent generations are not entering the field in large enough numbers to fill replacement needs. For years, educators, the media, and others in the United States and some other countries have sent the message that a four-year degree was the only path to a well-paying and rewarding career. Salary statistics that show electricians earn salaries that match, or even exceed, those of people in some white-collar professions demonstrate that this belief is false.

■ *There is a shortage of electricians in Canada.*

But back to the employment picture. There is a worldwide shortage of electricians and other skilled trades workers, according to the human resource consulting firm ManpowerGroup. Globally, workers in the skilled trades were cited by employers as the most in-demand occupational field. By continent/region, skilled trades workers topped the most in-demand list in the Americas, Europe, the Middle East, and Africa. They ranked fourth in the Asia-Pacific region. The top reasons globally that employer can't find talent are lack of available applicants, lack of technical competence, and lack of experience.

The recruitment firm Michael Page recently conducted research to determine deman for specific careers by country. It found that there is a shortage of electricians in Norway, Russia, Canada, Australia and New Zealand.

■ *Electricians who also know how to install and service solar panels will have especially strong j prospects.*

Many electricians are approaching retirement age, which is creating many new opportunities for young electricians.

Demand for electricians is also strong in the United States. Job opportunities for electricians are expected to grow by 14 percent during the next decade, according to the U.S. Department of Labor (USDL). This is much faster than the average growth (7 percent) expected for all occupations. The USDL says that "electricians who can perform many different tasks, such as electronic systems repair, solar photovoltaic installation, and industrial component wiring should have the best job opportunities. In addition, workers with military service experience are viewed favorably during initial hiring." There will be many new jobs for electricians because of the following factors:

- Many electricians are approaching retirement age. It's estimated that about 25 percent of today's electricians are age fifty-five or over, and there are currently not enough trainees to fill replacement needs.

- The construction industry has bounced back after the **Great Recession**, and demand is growing for electricians on new construction projects. Job opportunities for electricians in the construction industry are expected to grow by 19 percent during the next decade. Especially strong demand will occur in utility system construction and with electrical contractors and other wiring installation contractors.

- Technology of all types is becoming more prevalent in homes and businesses, and electricians will be needed to install new wiring and upgrade or service existing electrical wiring and components.

- Companies are in increasing need of electricians to help install new electrical systems in manufacturing plants, and maintain older equipment.

- The alternative energy (solar, wind, geothermal, hydropower, biomass) sector is enjoying strong growth, and electricians will be needed, especially in the solar and wind industries, to help install and service photovoltaic arrays, wind turbines, and related components. As more consumers utilize alternative energy resources, electricians will be needed to connect these sources to homes and power grids.

- There is a growing emphasis on energy efficiency by consumers, corporations, and government agencies. Electricians are needed to help replace energy-sucking systems and equipment and to conduct energy audits.

- The number of people and businesses that are installing **smart home technology**—a system of interconnected devices that perform certain actions to save energy, time, and money—continues to rise. In fact, the United States has the highest smart home technology penetration rate, followed by Japan and Germany, according to Statista.com. It's estimated that the global smart home market will reach a value of more than $40 billion in just a few years' time, and electricians will be needed to install and service these systems.

■ *Learn how scientists convert solar energy into electricity.*

Women in the Electrical Trades

Although women comprise about 47 percent of the U.S. workforce, only 1.5 percent of electricians are female. Industry leaders and associations are trying to increase the number of women entering this exciting and rewarding field by hosting informational events, founding support groups, and establishing mentorship programs. Here are a few organizations that exist to support women in the electrical trades and the construction industry:

The International Brotherhood of Electrical Workers' Electrical Workers Minority Caucus (http:// www.ibew-ewmc.com) seeks to promote equal opportunity and employment for women and ethnic minorities by offering membership, a leadership conference, and other resources.

The National Electrical Contractors Association (NECA, http://www.necanet.org/neca-community/peer-groups/women-in-neca) offers a Women In NECA forum.

The National Association of Women in Construction (NAWIC, http//www.nawic.org) offers membership, an annual meeting, and scholarships. It also publishes *The NAWIC IMAGE*.

The Canadian Association of Women in Construction (http://www.cawic.ca) offers membership, a mentoring program, networking events, and a job bank at its website.

■ *View interviews with women electricians.*

New Technologies

Electricians are increasingly becoming high-tech workers. Gone are the days of basi hands-on training for electrical apprentices. Today, electricians need strong comput skills to be able to install and service building and manufacturing systems that are run by complex systems that incorporate computer processors, fiber optics, sophis-ticated controllers, complex sensors, and, at times, *artificial intelligence*. As a result, apprentices in many programs need their own laptop computers, and some union training centers have computer labs for apprentices to view training simula-tions and practice operating local area networks and the software that controls thes complicated systems. Some electrical contractors are even creating their own traini facilities to educate their workers about the technical aspects of the job.

Electrical contractors must also master the use of office management software suc as Microsoft Excel and Word, and develop skill at using the internet and social med to attract and interact with customers. Some contractors are using live video tech-nology to communicate with customers and troubleshoot basic electrical problems. Electrical contractors also use building information modeling software, a computer application that uses a 3D model-based process to more efficiently plan, design, build, and manage buildings and infrastructure.

These are just a few of the technologies that are changing the work of electricians. you're interested in becoming an electrician, you should become familiar with these

The construction industry has created many programs to increase the number of female electricians. A female electrician calibrates an electrical socket.

technologies, as well as keep an eye out for emerging technologies and the use of electricity and electrical systems in new products ranging from smart homes to electric vehicles.

Challenges to Employment Growth

Although job prospects for electricians are currently strong, a few factors may slow employment growth. If another significant economic recession occurs, funding for construction projects will decrease, consumers will spend less money (which will cause companies to produce fewer goods), and the public, businesses, and government agencies may spend less money on new projects and electrical upgrades. As a result, fewer electricians will be needed.

Demand for electricians will also be influenced by government policy. If the government funds more infrastructure, alternative energy, and energy efficiency projects, there will be more need for electricians. On the other hand, cuts in funding for these areas may limit new opportunities for electricians.

The emergence of smart building technology is both a boon and a potential bane to electricians. While this technology has created new opportunities for electricians, the logical evolution of this technology—combined with quickly evolving artificial intelligence—suggests that these systems may become so automated and issue-free that an electrician may never be required to visit the site—except for the initial installation.

Finally, while there is a current shortage of electricians worldwide, supply and demand in all careers ebbs and flows. As governments provide more funding for electrical apprenticeship training programs, the media continues to spotlight the benefits of working in the trades, and people begin to recognize that a career as an electrician is a good-paying alternative to occupations that require a four-year degree, the number of electricians may gradually grow to exceed demand. But this is just a potential future, and current demand for electricians is extremely strong.

In Closing

Is a career as an electrician a good fit for you? If you like working both with your hands and with technology; like the fact that no day on the job is the same as any other; and enjoy using your skills and talents to help others, the answer is yes. And the good pay (top earners in the U.S. make $90,000 or more annually) and strong employment prospects worldwide make this career an appealing option for those wh

Employment for electricians—especially in the construction industry—will slow if there is another economic recession.

don't want to pursue a four-year degree. I hope that you'll use this book as a starting point to discover even more about a career as an electrician. Talk to electricians about their careers and shadow them on the job, use the resources of professional organizations, and try out electrical projects at home to learn more about the field. Good luck on your career exploration!

■ *The future is bright for skilled electricians.*

Did You Know?

- About 629,000 electricians are employed in the United States. Sixty-three percent work in the electrical contractors and other wiring installation contractors industry.

- Approximately 10 percent of electricians are self-employed.

- About 9 percent of workers in the construction industry are women.

Source: U.S. Department of Labor

Text-Dependent Questions

Why is employment strong for electricians?

What types of technology do electricians use to do their jobs?

What are some developments that might slow employment for electricians?

Research Project

earn more about solar power by visiting http://www.seia.org/about/solar-energy and tps://www.bls.gov/green/solar_power. Write a report about the benefits of using lar energy and present it to your class.

Series Glossary of Key Terms

apprentice: A trainee who is enrolled in a program that prepares them to work as a skilled trades worker. Apprentices must complete 2,000 hours of on-the-job training and 144 hours of related classroom instruction during a four- to five-year course of study. They are paid a salary that increases as they obtain experience.

apprenticeship: A formal training program that often consists of 2,000 hours of on-the-job training and 144 hours of related classroom instruction per year for four t five years.

bid: A formal offer created by a contractor or trades worker that details the work tha will be done, the amount the company or individual will charge, and the time frame i which the work will be completed.

blueprints: A reproduction of a technical plan for the construction of a home or oth structure. Blueprints are created by licensed architects.

building codes: A series of rules established by local, state, regional, and national governments that ensure safe construction. The National Electrical Code, which was developed by the National Fire Protection Association, is an example of a building code in the United States.

building information modeling software: A computer application that uses a 3D model-based process that helps construction, architecture, and engineering professionals to more efficiently plan, design, build, and manage buildings and infra structure.

building materials: Any naturally-occurring (clay, rocks, sand, wood, etc.) or human-made substances (steel, cement, etc.) that are used to construct buildings and other structures.

building permit: Written permission from a government entity that allows trades workers to construct, alter, or otherwise work at a construction site.

community college: A private or public two-year college that awards certificates an associate degrees.

general contractor: A licensed individual or company that accepts primary respon- sibility for work done at a construction site or in another setting.

green construction: The planning, design, construction, and operation of structures an environmentally responsible manner. Green construction stresses energy and ater efficiency, the use of eco-friendly construction materials (when possible), indoor nvironmental quality, and the structure's overall effects on its site or the larger ommunity. Also known as **green building**.

inspection: The process of reviewing/examining ongoing or recently completed onstruction work to ensure that it has been completed per the applicable building odes. Construction and building inspectors are employed by government agencies nd private companies that provide inspection services to potential purchasers of ew construction or remodeled buildings.

job foreman: A journeyman (male or female) who manages a group of other jour-eymen and apprentices on a project.

journeyman: A trades worker who has completed an apprenticeship training. If censed, he or she can work without direct supervision, but, for large projects, must ork under permits issued to a master electrician.

Leadership in Energy and Environmental Design (LEED) certification: A third-arty verification that remodeled or newly constructed buildings have met the highest iteria for water efficiency, energy efficiency, the use of eco-friendly materials and uilding practices, indoor environmental quality, and other criteria. LEED certification the most popular green building rating system in the world.

master trades worker: A trades professional who has a minimum level of expe-ence (usually at least three to four years as a licensed professional) and who has assed an examination. Master trades workers manage journeymen, trades workers, nd apprentices.

prefabricated: The manufacture or fabrication of certain components of a structure valls, electrical components, etc.) away from the construction site. Prefabricated oducts are brought to the construction site and joined with existing structures or omponents.

schematic diagram: An illustration of the components of a system that uses bstract, graphic symbols instead of realistic pictures or illustrations.

self-employment: Working for oneself as a small business owner, rather than for a orporation or other employer. Self-employed people are responsible for generating eir own income, and they must provide their own fringe benefits (such as health nsurance).

smart home technology: A system of interconnected devices that perform certain actions to save energy, time, and money.

technical college: A public or private college that offers two- or four-year programs in practical subjects, such as the trades, information technology, applied sciences, agriculture, and engineering.

union: An organization that seeks to gain better wages, benefits, and working conditions for its members. Also called a **labor union** or **trade union**.

zoning permit: A document issued by a government body that stipulates that the project in question meets existing zoning rules for a geographic area.

zoning rules: Restrictions established by government bodies as to what type of structure can be built in a certain area. For example, many cities have zoning rules that restrict the construction of factories in residential areas.

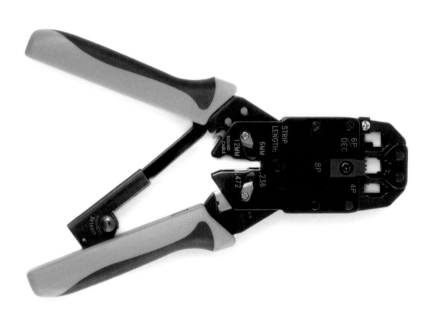

Index

Photo Credits

Further Reading & Internet Resources

Hawthorne, Nigel. *Tesla Vs Edison: The Life-Long Feud that Electrified the World.* London, U.K.: Chartwell Books, 2016.

Geier, Michael Jay. *How to Diagnose and Fix Everything Electronic.* 2nd ed. New York: McGraw-Hill Education, 2015.

Gibilisco, Stan, and Simon Monk. *Teach Yourself Electricity and Electronics.* 6th ed. New York: McGraw-Hill Education, 2016.

Graves, Colleen, and Aaron Graves. *The Big Book of Makerspace Projects: Inspiring Makers to Experiment, Create, and Learn.* New York: McGraw-Hill Education, 2016.

Sherman, Pat. *Electricity.* New York: Cavendish Square Publishing, 2017.

Internet Resources

https://www.bls.gov/ooh/construction-and-extraction/electricians. htm#tab-4: This article from the *Occupational Outlook Handbook* provides information on job duties, educational requirements, salaries, and the employment outlook for electricians.

http://www.byf.org: This web initiative of the National Center for Construction Education and Research offers overviews of more than thirty careers in the trades, videos of trades workers on the job, and much more.

http://www.explorethetrades.org/electrical: Explore the Trades provides answers to questions such as What is an Electrician?, Why Become an Electrician?, and What is an Electrician Apprentice?

http://www.myelectriccareer.com: This website, which is sponsored by Independent Electrical Contractors, touts the benefits of working as an electrician and provides information on training opportunities.

http://www.necanet.org/professional-development/careers-in-electrical-contracting: Visit this website (which is sponsored by the National Electrical Contractors Association) to learn about the duties of electrical contractors and training opportunities.

About the Author

Andrew Morkes has been a writer and editor for more than 25 years. He is the autho of more than 20 books about college-planning and careers, including many titles in this series, the *Vault Career Guide to Social Media*, and *They Teach That in College!? A Resource Guide to More Than 100 Interesting College Majors*, which was selected as one of the best books of the year by the library journal *Voice of Youth Advocates*. He is also the author and publisher of "The Morkes Report: College and Career Planning Trends" blog.

Video Credits

Chapter 1:

An electrician at a job site discusses his job duties, necessary skills, and work environment: http://x-qr.net/1FQh

Check out electricians working in a variety of jobs: http://x-qr.net/1G3Z

Three experienced electricians talk about the rewards of becoming an electrician: http://x-qr.net/1HWj

Chapter 4:

View interviews with several apprentices and learn about classroom and hands-on requirements for apprentices: http://x-qr.net/1GLd

Watch an apprentice at work and learn about the strong salaries and steady deman for electricians: http://x-qr.net/1HKo

Chapter 5:

Get some hands-on experience by learning how to measure voltage: http://x-qr.net/1CqS

Build a basic electrical generator at home: http://x-qr.net/1Dis

Chapter 6:

Learn how scientists convert solar energy into electricity: http://x-qr.net/1HMT

View interviews with women electricians: http://x-qr.net/1Egz